DATE DUE

Countries Around the World

Italy

Claire Throp

Heinemann Library
Chicago, Illinois

www.heinemannraintree.com
Visit our website to find out more information about Heinemann-Raintree books.

To order:
☎ Phone 888-454-2279
🖥 Visit www.heinemannraintree.com to browse our catalog and order online.

Edited by Louise Galpine, Kate DeVilliers, and Laura Knowles
Designed by Richard Parker
Original illustrations © Capstone Global Library Ltd 2011
Illustrated by Oxford Designers & Illustrators
Picture research by Liz Alexander
Originated by Capstone Global Library Ltd
Printed in China by CTPS

15 14 13 12 11
10 9 8 7 6 5 4 3 2 1

Library of Congress Cataloging-in-Publication Data
Throp, Claire.
  Italy / Claire Throp.
    p. cm.—(Countries around the world)
  Includes bibliographical references and index.
  ISBN 978-1-4329-5210-5 (hc)—ISBN 978-1-4329-5235-8 (pb) 1.
Italy—Juvenile literature. 2. Italy—History—Juvenile literature. I.
Title.
  DG417.T49 2012
  945—dc22   2010044774

Acknowledgments
We would like to thank the following for permission to reproduce photographs: Alamy pp. **18** (© blickwinkel), **27** (© Liam White), **30** (© dbimages); Corbis pp. **9** (© Summerfield Press), **21** (© Ciro Fusco/epa), **32** (© Tim de Waele), **33** (© Stephane Reix/For Picture), **34** (© Ada Masella /Immaginazione); iStockphoto p. **31** (© Jens Fiskbaek); Photolibrary pp. **10** (DEA PICTURE LIBRARY), **16** (PH+), **22** (Antonello Lanzellotto), **24** (David H. Wells/Aurora Photos); Shutterstock pp. **5** (© Natalia Barsukova), **6** (© wjarek), **11** (© Christina Solodukhina), **13** (© jordache), **14** (© Dan Breckwoldt), **15** (© Guryanov Andrey Vladimirovich), **17** (© Roca), **19** (© Roberto Zilli), **29** (© M. Unal Ozmen), **35** (© melodija), **37** (© Brian A Jackson), **39** (© SF photo), **46** (© Route66).

Cover photograph of gondolas passing on narrow canal in Venice reproduced with permission of Photolibrary/Chad Ehlers/Nordic Photos.

We would like to thank Rob Bowden for his invaluable help in the preparation of this book.

Every effort has been made to contact copyright holders of material reproduced in this book. Any omissions will be rectified in subsequent printings if notice is given to the publisher.

Disclaimer
All the Internet addresses (URLs) given in this book were valid at the time of going to press. However, due to the dynamic nature of the Internet, some addresses may have changed, or sites may have changed or ceased to exist since publication. While the author and publisher regret any inconvenience this may cause readers, no responsibility for any such changes can be accepted by either the author or the publisher.

Contents

Some words are printed in bold, **like this**. You can find out what they mean by looking in the glossary.

Introducing Italy

What comes to mind when you think of Italy? Food such as pizza, pasta, and ice cream? Soccer? Fashion? Family? Or artists such as Michelangelo? Italy is famous for all these things and more. Italy is a country in southern Europe that is recognizable because it looks like a high-heeled boot. It is a **peninsula**. A peninsula is a long, thin stretch of land that sticks out into the sea. Italy lies in the Mediterranean Sea, and is about the same size as the state of Arizona.

Daily life

Shake hands once and say *buongiorno* (good day) when you first meet an Italian. You can also ask *come stai?* (how are you?). You should shake hands again when you say goodbye. You shouldn't use the greeting *ciao* (pronounced "chow") unless you know the person.

Population and language

About 60 million people live in Italy. The national language is Italian. Italian is a Romance language. It is called this because it is based on Latin, a very old language that the Romans spoke nearly 3,000 years ago.

Repubblica Italiana is the proper name for Italy in the Italian language. Italians also call their country *Belpaese*, which means "beautiful country."

Only recently single

Italy has only been a **unified** (single) country since 1871. Before that, it was a collection of **states** or regions that often fought each other and other countries. The fact that these regions were separate for so long is probably why there are still big differences in **culture**, food, and lifestyle throughout Italy.

Capri is an island off the south coast of the Gulf of Naples. It has been a popular vacation spot since Roman times.

History: Toward Unity

The Etruscans were the most powerful people in Italy before the Romans. No one is sure where they came from, but it is thought that by the 700s BCE they were in control of northern and central Italy. They were an advanced **civilization**. They built walls around cities, dug ditches for watering their crops, and had governments ruled by kings.

The Greeks were in control of southern Italy. They built beautiful temples, such as those still standing at Agrigento.

The Romans

The Roman **Republic** was set up in 509 BCE. It gradually became a huge power, controlling **trade** routes. However, it was often not very **stable**, as different groups fought each other.

According to legend, Rome was founded by the twin sons of the god Mars, Romulus and Remus, who were raised by a wolf. Romulus is supposed to have killed his twin and made himself the first king of Rome in 753 BCE.

Building an empire

The Roman **Empire** lasted for hundreds of years, from 49 BCE when Julius Caesar came to power, to 476 CE. The Golden Age of Rome (known as Pax Romana), a 200-year period of peace, saw the Romans invent roads, public baths, and flushing toilets.

German **tribes** brought the Golden Age of empire to an end in 476 CE. Parts of Italy were taken over by tribes, such as the Goths and the Franks.

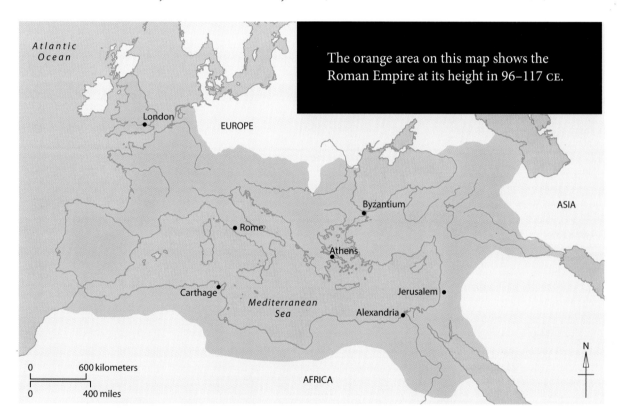

The orange area on this map shows the Roman Empire at its height in 96–117 CE.

Daily life

If you were an Italian 2,000 years ago, you might have gone to see gladiator fights in places like the Colosseum in Rome. Men would fight each other, as well as animals. In 80 CE games were held for 100 days and nights. More than 5,000 animals were killed.

City-states

For hundreds of years Italy was not a united country. The north was dominated by the **Holy Roman Empire** and the **pope**. Gradually city-states, such as Venice and Florence, became more powerful. In the south, French rulers, such as the Normans and later the Bourbons, held power.

The Renaissance

The **Renaissance** in Italy began in the early 1300s and reintroduced ancient Greek and Roman ideas about art and **culture**. Florence, under the rule of the Medici family, produced and encouraged great artists such as Botticelli and Michelangelo.

A united Italy?

In 1796, a French general, Napoleon Bonaparte, invaded Italy. Under Napoleon the Italian **states** were ruled as one country for the first time. The former foreign rulers of Italy, including the Holy Roman Emperor and the Bourbons, took control again when Napoleon was defeated in 1815. However, some people called for Italy to be freed from foreign control and united as one country.

Giuseppe Garibaldi took part in the campaigns for **unification**. In 1860 he took 1,000 volunteers known as the Red Shirts to free Naples and Sicily from their foreign rulers. By 1871, Italy was a united country.

ANTONIO VIVALDI (1678–1741)

The composer and violinist Vivaldi was born in Venice. He was known as "Il prete rosso," which means "the red priest." This was because he trained as a priest and had red hair! His most famous piece is "The Four Seasons."

In his painting *The Adoration of the Magi* (1475), Sandro Botticelli included himself (on the right in the yellow robe) and Lorenzo de Medici. Lorenzo is on the left with his hands resting on his sword.

Two World Wars

Italy backed the **Allies** in World War I (1914–1918), but was disappointed not to get the land it had been promised at the end of the war. Benito Mussolini founded the Fascist party, a **nationalist** political party, in 1919. He was asked to form a government in 1922. It was under Mussolini that the Vatican City was recognized as an independent state.

In World War II (1939–1945), Mussolini made a deal with Adolf Hitler, Germany's leader, so Italy fought against the Allies. However, in 1943, the Italian king had Mussolini arrested. Germany helped him escape and set him up as leader of northern Italy. Northern Italy was not freed until April 1945. Mussolini was later shot while trying to escape.

Mussolini called himself "*Il Duce,*" which means "leader."

In 2002 the Italian **currency**, the lira, was replaced by the euro. The euro is also used in many other European countries.

Italy becomes a republic

In 1946 the monarchy ended, and Italy became a republic. Italy was a founding member of what later became the **European Union (EU)** when it signed the Treaty of Rome in 1957.

More than 60 governments have ruled Italy in the years since the war. In the late 1960s, strikes and protests occurred in Italy. Organized crime groups, such as the Mafia, became more powerful. However, Italy's **economy** became one of the strongest in Europe.

In the 1990s, Italy became famous for **corruption**. Members of the government and business leaders were forced to leave their jobs because of financial scandals. Only recently have things become more stable, although the global financial crisis in 2008 badly affected Italy.

Regions and Resources: Mountains and Lakes

Italy has borders with four countries: France, Switzerland, Austria, and Slovenia. It is surrounded by five seas, which are the Mediterranean, Adriatic, Ionian, the Tyrrhenian, and the Ligurian.

Sicily and Sardinia are islands that are part of Italy. There are also a lot of smaller Italian islands. Sicily is the largest island in the Mediterranean Sea. Sardinia is made up of mountains pushing up from the sea.

Italy is unusual because within the country there are two independent **states**. San Marino is in the east of Italy and is popular with tourists. The Vatican City is in Rome and covers less than 0.6 square miles (1 square kilometer) .

Italy has over 4,970 miles (8,000 kilometers) of coastline.

Climate

The climate in Italy is varied. The country can be divided into three main areas. The Po Valley in the northeast has hot summers and cold winters. It also has the Bora, a strong, cold wind that blows across the northeast in winter. In the northern, alpine area, summer is the rainy season and there can be a lot of storms. In the rest of Italy, coastal areas are usually hotter than inland areas.

Lakes

Lakes in Italy are common places for vacations, but many people live there all year round. The largest is Lake Garda. Despite this, another lake has the name Lake Maggiore. *Maggiore* means "greater." Lake Como in the north is the deepest lake.

Lake Garda covers 143 square miles (370 square kilometers).

How to say...

island	*l'isola*	(lee-so-la)
sea	*il mare*	(eel MA-re)
river	*fiume*	(fee-oo-may)
mountain	*montagna*	(mon-tan-ya)
lake	*lago*	(la-go)
volcano	*vulcano*	(vul-ca-no)

Rivers

The Po is the longest river in Italy, at 390 miles (628 kilometers). The Po Valley area is good for farming. The Tiber River flows through Rome, and in Roman times it had ten bridges. The Arno River runs through Tuscany and regularly floods. In 1966, a large flood killed 40 people and damaged many works of art and rare books.

Mountains

More than three-quarters of Italy is made up of mountains. The Alps in the north stretch from east to west. Italy's highest point is at the top of Monte Bianco de Courmayeur, which is 2,950 feet (4,748 meters) high. The Dolomites in the east have beautiful scenery. The Apennines are known as the "backbone" of Italy because they run down the center of the country.

In 2009 the Dolomites were added to the UNESCO World Heritage list. UNESCO tries to protect areas of the world that are of outstanding beauty or importance.

Mount Etna is on the island of Sicily and is the largest volcano in Europe. This house was buried during one of its eruptions.

Volcanoes

A fault line is a crack in Earth's crust. A fault line runs down the middle of Italy and can cause earthquakes and produce active volcanoes. Vesuvius, Etna, and Stromboli are all active volcanoes, so they could **erupt** at any time. Etna and Stromboli are on islands, and both erupted in 2010.

Mount Vesuvius is south of Naples. Nearly 2,000 years ago the volcano erupted and covered the city of Pompeii in ash. It happened so quickly that people were killed instantly. Casts of their bodies made by the ash can still be seen today. Since then Vesuvius has erupted more than 30 times, most recently in 1944. Many thousands of people live near the volcano and would be in danger if it erupted again.

Resources and trade

Italy has some natural **resources**, but natural gas and salt are among the most important. The country has to **import** four-fifths of its energy. About 60 percent of Italy's **trade** is with other EU countries. Meat and dairy foods are imported. **Exports** include food products such as olive oil and tomatoes. Italy also exports clothing, cars, and machinery.

The Fiat car company has factories in Turin, in northwest Italy.

Economy

The euro has been Italy's **currency** since 2002. Italy has the fourth largest **economy** in Europe, but it was badly affected by the global economic crisis that began in 2008. It was one of the first countries to go into a **recession**. A recession is when the economy slows down, people spend less, and unemployment rises.

Jobs

The north of Italy is **industrialized** and wealthy, while the south is more agricultural and less well off. Nearly 70 percent of Italians live in cities. The main jobs are in office work, tourism, and fashion.

In **rural** areas, farming is common. Crops include grapes and olives. Rural tourism is becoming very popular. People stay in farmhouses called *agriturismos* and get to experience life in a real Italian household, as well as local festivals and traditions.

Agriculture
4.2%

Industry
30.7%

Services
65.1%

This pie chart shows that most Italian jobs are in services. This includes jobs in tourism.

Women in work

Women have been taking a more active part in the economy in recent years, particularly in the north. Traditionally women were housewives, but after World War II many took up careers. Some people think women's focus on their careers is why Italy's **birth rate** has fallen.

Italy is one of the world's largest producers of grapes.

Wildlife: Increasing Environmental Awareness

There are many different types of wildlife to be found in Italy, particularly in the national parks.

About 800,000 people have a hunting licence in Italy. In the past, hunting has led to **species** becoming extinct (dying out) or **endangered**. In 1992 a law was passed that only allows hunting in certain places, in order to protect rare animals.

Species such as red deer, roe deer, and pink flamingos used to be rare. Today there are thousands of pink flamingos on lagoons along the coast, and over 1,000 red deer in the Monte Arcosu Oasis on the island of Sardinia alone. Other species, such as the brown bear and the bearded vulture, are being reintroduced to the Italian countryside.

In the 1970s there were about 100 wolves in Italy, but now the number has increased to between 500 and 600.

This is an *Orchis morio*, one of the many kinds of orchid that grow in Italy.

Plants and trees

In the Maiella Mountains, 60 species of orchid can be found—the largest number of orchid species in Europe. Oak, cork, and pine are the most common trees.

How to say...

bear	*l'orso*	(LAW-so)
deer	*cervo*	(CHAIR-vo)
toad	*rospo*	(ROS-po)
wolf	*lupo*	(LOO-po)

Toads predict earthquake!

In 2009, an earthquake struck L'Aquila in central Italy. Scientists have since discovered that about 96 percent of male toads abandoned their **breeding** ground five days before the earthquake. The number of toads breeding together dropped to zero three days before the disaster. Scientists think that toads can sense when an earthquake is about to happen, perhaps by gases being released from the earth. Normally toads would remain at the breeding site until their young are born.

National parks

There are 24 national parks in Italy, which cover about five percent of the country. National parks are important for helping to protect Italy's animals and plants. People can visit the parks, and some include towns within their boundaries.

Environmental issues

Today Italians are more interested in the environment. This is partly due to climate change and pollution problems, particularly in the towns and cities of the more **industrialized** north. Much of the pollution comes from vehicles. Italy has one of the highest numbers of cars per person in the world. People are being encouraged to use their vehicles less often. Some local governments are considering a **congestion charge** similar to that used in London.

Waste problems

More than 110,230 tons (100,000 tonnes) of garbage filled the streets of Naples in early 2008. It was piled up in front of schools, causing health fears as children were about to return to school after Christmas. Trash collection had stopped because the local **landfill site** was full, and an incinerator for burning garbage was not completed. The army had to help get rid of the waste.

YOUNG PEOPLE

Green Cross International (GCI) is a worldwide organization that was set up in 1993. The Earth Charter Youth Contest, organized by GCI, aims to help children understand a different environmental issue every year. In 2009, around 30,000 Italian students took part. The winners' schools receive money that must be put into environmental projects, which the children can choose.

In the past 15 years, the Italian government has spent more than $2 billion trying to sort out the waste problem in Naples.

Infrastructure: Republican Government

Italy is a **republic**. This means that the people can vote for the politicians they want to represent them. In Italy the **head of state** is a president. He or she is **elected** every seven years by parliament and representatives from the regions. The president can call special sessions of parliament, delay laws, and command the military. The prime minister is the leader of the government and runs the country on a day-to-day level. He or she is chosen by the president, often from a list suggested by the strongest political parties.

There are two **assemblies** in the Italian parliament: the Senate and the Chamber of Deputies. The Senate has 315 members, known as senators, and there are 630 deputies. Parliament must be elected at least every five years, although elections often happen more frequently than this.

The Chamber of Deputies meets in the Palazzo Montecitorio in Rome.

Voting

Italian **citizens** can vote in elections for the Chamber of Deputies when they are 18 years old, but they must be 25 or over to vote for representatives in the Senate. More people in Italy vote in elections than anywhere else in Europe.

Regions

Italy is divided into 20 regions, five of which have special powers. Sardinia and Valle d'Aosta, for example, have more control over their region's government. Other regions do not have very much independence from central government.

European Union

Italy was one of the founding members of the **European Union (EU)**. Italians have been strongly in favor of the EU ever since.

FRANCE
GERMANY
SLOVAKIA
AUSTRIA
SWITZERLAND
LIECHTENSTEIN
TRENTINO-ALTO ADIGE
FRIULI-VENEZIA GIULIA
HUNGARY
VALLE D'AOSTA
Aosta
Milan
Trento
SLOVENIA
Turin
LOMBARDY
VENETO
Trieste
Venice
PIEDMONT
EMILIA ROMAGNA
CROATIA
Genoa
LIGURIA
Bologna
BOSNIA-HERZEGOVINA
Florence
SAN MARINO
Ancona
TUSCANY
Perugia
MARCHE
UMBRIA
LAZIO
L'Aquila
VATICAN
Rome
ABRUZZO
MOLISE
Campobosso
SARDINIA
CAMPANIA
Bari
Naples
Potenza
PUGLIA
BASILICATA
Cagliari
CALABRIA
Palermo
Catanzaro
SICILY
N
TUNISIA

0   100   200 kilometers
0   100   200 miles

This map shows the regions of Italy with their capitals. It also includes the independent **states** of San Marino and the Vatican.

Police and military

Several different branches of the police exist in Italy. They include the state police force, which deals with thefts and visa problems for visitors. The carabinieri are part of the army. They deal with serious crime and public order. The carabinieri are common throughout Italy, even in the smallest villages. They are the best-funded police force in Italy and sometimes even get to use helicopters and speed boats!

Italy has an army, air force, and navy. About $37 billion is spent on the military each year, including the carabinieri. Italy is a member of the North Atlantic Treaty Organization (NATO), and a number of NATO military bases are found in the country.

These railroad policemen in Florence are using personal transport vehicles. The vehicles allow the police a better view of the area because they are 10 inches (25 centimeters) off the ground.

Media

There are few national newspapers in Italy because most are focused on the regions. Examples of daily newspapers include Milan's *Il Giorno* and Rome's *Il Messaggero*. Rai is the public television service, but at times it has been influenced by politics. The country's prime minister, Silvio Berlusconi, owns and controls the major private television stations.

Health

Italy's National Health Service is a free service that was established in 1978 and developed in the 1990s to improve patient care. Most people are covered by a government system that provides payments in case of accident, illness, or unemployment. The World Health Organization has ranked Italy second in the world for their health care system.

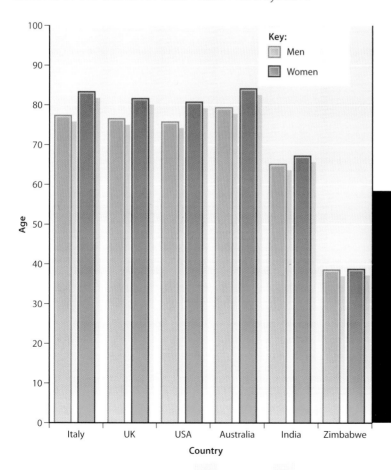

Italians are generally healthy, partly due to their low-fat diet. They have one of the highest life expectancies in the world. This bar chart shows how Italy's life expectancy figures measure against those in other countries.

YOUNG PEOPLE

Italian children spend their spare time in the same way as many other European children: playing computer games, watching television, meeting friends in parks, shopping, or going to the movies. They like to spend time with their families, too.

School structure

Do you ever wonder what school is like in other countries? Do they have to wear uniforms? What kind of subjects do they study? Are there large classes?

In Italy children must go to elementary school from the age of six to eleven. They study similar subjects to those of children in any other country, such as math, history, and science. There are normally no more than 25 children in a class.

Middle school lasts for three years, up to the age of 14. A **national curriculum** is followed, but some schools have extra classes in the afternoon in subjects such as sports or music. Some children go home for lunch.

After taking exams at age 14, children have to make some decisions about what they want to continue studying. The next level of schooling is focused on particular subjects. Teenagers can choose to go to a more academic school or to an arts, technical, or language school.

Daily life

Some children in Italy go to school six days a week, from 8:30 a.m. to 1:30 p.m. This means they have to go to school on Saturdays! In big cities, however, children often go to school for full days. Italian schoolchildren also have long summer vacations, from mid-June to mid-September—that's three months!

Students often wear overalls rather than a uniform. Some children are allowed to wear their everyday clothes.

Culture: From Food to Festivals

Italians are known for loving their food. Each region has its own special recipes, but pasta, pizza, and ice cream are just some of the delights Italy is famous for. Italians tend to shop for food each day. Food markets are common, as the food is generally fresher and cheaper than in a supermarket. The Slow Food Movement began in Italy. This encourages people to buy their food locally.

Italians eat out frequently. Children often go, too, even if the meal is eaten late at night. However, lunch is traditionally the longest and most important meal of the day. Italians often have three courses at lunchtime, followed by coffee.

Daily life

Italians know that someone is a tourist if they order milky coffee, such as a cappuccino, late in the day. In Italy milky coffee is only drunk in the morning. Many Italians drink their morning coffee and eat their breakfast pastries standing up at the counter in a café.

Cinema and television

Going to the cinema is a common pastime in Italy. The majority of films are foreign-language films, usually in English, so they are **dubbed** into Italian. Famous Italian film stars include Anna Magnani, Sophia Loren, and Marcello Mastroianni. However, many Italians are just as likely to stay at home and watch television! Italians watch about four hours of television on average each day.

Vanilla ice cream

This recipe may not be as good as real Italian ice cream, but it will still taste great! Ask an adult to help you.

Ingredients

- 2 cups heavy cream
- ⅓ cup sugar
- 3 egg yolks
- 2 vanilla pods

What to do

1. Cut the vanilla pods in half lengthways and remove the seeds.
2. Pour the cream into a pan and add the pods. Bring it to a boil.
3. Add the sugar to the cream and stir it until the sugar dissolves.
4. Whisk the egg yolks together in a big bowl. Stir continuously as you add the cream.
5. Pour the mixture into another bowl through a sieve. Mix in the vanilla pod seeds.
6. Place the mixture into a freezer-proof container. It should take about two hours to set.

YOUNG PEOPLE

The singles download charts in Italy include many non-Italian acts, including Cheryl Cole, Kylie Minogue, and Ne-Yo. Italian teenagers have their own idols, though, such as Marco Carta. He is an Italian singer who won the Best Artist award at the San Remo Italian Music Festival in 2009. His song "*La Forza Mia*" ("My Strength") went to number one.

Opera

Many Italians love a type of musical play called opera. Opera began in Italy, but soon spread to other countries. The first opera, *Dafne*, was performed in Florence in 1598. La Scala in Milan is probably the world's best-known opera house.

La Scala was built between 1776 and 1778. It can seat 2,000 people.

The Bridge of Sighs in Venice was built in 1600. Its name comes from the prisoners who traveled across it on their way to prison. They used to sigh at their last sight of freedom.

Art and architecture

Many Italian cities, particularly Florence, are well known for having some of the best art and **architecture** in the world. One of the most famous art galleries, the Uffizi, is in Florence. In Rome there are paintings by Caravaggio, and Roman buildings to visit. In Vicenza (Venice) you can see buildings designed by the great architect, Andrea Palladio.

Literature

Dante Alighieri is one of Italy's best-known writers. He is famous for a long poem called *The Divine Comedy*, written between 1308 and 1321. It was written in the language of Tuscany rather than Latin, the usual written language at the time. Tuscan eventually became the common language of Italy. Other famous Italian writers include Umberto Eco and Elsa Morante.

Fashion

Italians take fashion very seriously. Twice a year, fashion shows are put on in Milan. Prada and Armani are two well-known Italian fashion labels.

GIORGIO ARMANI (BORN 1934)

Giorgio Armani was born in Piacenza in the north of Italy. At first he wanted to work in medicine or photography, but eventually he realized fashion was his career. He set up his own company in 1974, and still designs clothes today.

Sports

Sports are even more popular than fashion. *La Gazzetta dello Sport* is by far the best-selling newspaper in Italy. Soccer is the national sport, and fans are passionate about it. The Italian national soccer team is known as the Azzurri (the "light blues"), after the color of the team shirts. Formula One Grand Prix motor racing, cycling (Giro d'Italia), swimming, and skiing are also popular.

Cyclists get to see some amazing sights during the Giro d'Italia race.

FRANCESCA SCHIAVONE (BORN 1980)

Francesca Schiavone was the first Italian woman tennis player to win a Grand Slam singles title when she won the French Open in 2010. She was born in Milan in 1980. She turned professional in 1998, which meant she could begin to earn money playing tennis.

The national anthem

The national anthem, "*Il canto degli Italiani*" ("The Song of the Italians"), is often sung at sporting events. Goffredo Mameli wrote the words in 1847, and Michele Novaro composed the music. It is also known as "Mameli's Hym" and "Brothers of Italy," which is the first line of the anthem. It only became the official anthem in 1946, when Italy became a **republic**. The first verse is:

Brothers of Italy,
Italy has awoken,
with Scipio's helmet
binding her head.
Where is Victory?
Let her bow down,
For God has made her
Rome's slave.

Francesca Schiavone proudly held up her trophy after winning the French Open tennis tournament in 2010.

Religion

Since 1984 Italy has had no official religion, but most Italians are Roman Catholic Christians. However, only about a third go to church regularly. Other religious groups in Italy include Muslims and Jews.

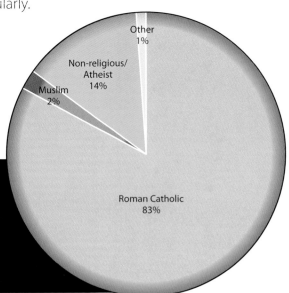

Other
1%

Non-religious/
Atheist
14%

Muslim
2%

Roman Catholic
83%

This chart shows the main religions practiced in Italy.

The Vatican in Rome is the home of the **pope**, the leader of the Roman Catholic Church. Many people attend Easter mass at the Vatican.

Every year in February, a ten-day **carnival** takes place in Venice. People dress up in colorful clothes and wear masks.

Festivals

Nearly every city, town, and village has an annual festival, many of which last for several days. They are often based on history or religion. In Siena, the Palio horse races take place in July and August. Riders from different parts of the city go around a very difficult course in the city's central square. Religious festivals often include a procession and feasting. One festival at Cocullo celebrates the local patron saint, Domenico. A statue of St. Domenico is carried along the streets covered in live snakes!

National holidays

Italy has twelve national holidays, including Liberation Day on April 25. This celebrates the freedom of Italy from German control in World War II. Other holidays are Easter Monday, All Saints' Day, and Christmas Day.

Italy Today

Italy is a country of varying landscapes, climate, and customs. This is due partly to the fact that the regions have only united as one country relatively recently. For many Italians, their loyalty is to their region rather than to their country. One of the few things that does seem to unify the whole country is sports, particularly soccer.

Family

Family is important to Italians of all ages. In 2000, almost 94 percent of Italian 15-year-olds said they ate their main meal with their family several times a week. This was more than in any other country.

However, at the moment Italy's **birth rate** is one of the lowest in Europe. It means that Italian families are not having as many children as they once did. Italians are now actually being encouraged to have more children.

Italian life

Italians love food, sports, festivals, and having fun! They have a high standard of living. The political situation in Italy is never very **stable**, with governments changing often, but this does not seem to affect Italians' love of life.

Daily life

Many Italians go for a stroll in the evening. This is something that happens all over Italy and is called *passeggiata*. People use the walk to meet friends, find out about local gossip, or even to show off new clothes! Often families go for walks together.

The Arno River divides the city of Florence. Florentines talk about north of the river as "over here" (*Arno di quà*) and the south as "over there" (*Arno di là*).

Fact File

Official country name: Republic of Italy

Official language: Italian, with minority French and German

Capital city: Rome

Bordering countries: France, Switzerland, Austria, and Slovenia

Government: Republic

Population: 60,340,000

Life expectancy at birth: 77.3 years for men; 83.3 years for women (ranked 13th in the world)

Religious majority: Roman Catholic

Area: 116,346 square miles (301,336 square kilometers)

Coastline: 4,971 miles (8,000 kilometers)

Longest river: River Po at 390 miles (628 kilometers)

Highest point: Mont Blanc at 15,771 feet (4,807 meters)

Currency: Euro (100 cents = 1 euro)

Natural resources: Coal, mercury, marble, natural gas and crude oil reserves, fish

Imports: Chemicals, transportation equipment, energy products, food

Exports: Machinery, chemicals, clothes, wine

Popularity as a tourist destination: Fifth in the world, with 43.7 million tourists in 2007

Festivals: *Carnevale* (February), *Corsa dei Ceri* (May—a race through Gubbio's streets with candles and statues), *Il Palio* (July and August), Venice International Film Festival (August), *Salone Internazionale del Gusto* (Slow Food festival held every other year in October)

Famous Italians:	Claudia Cardinale (actress), Andrea Palladio (architect), Caravaggio (artist), Fabio Cannavaro (soccer player), Giuseppe Verdi (composer), Galileo Galilei (astronomer), Cecilia Bartoli (opera singer)
National Holidays:	New Year's Day (January 1), Epiphany (January 6), Easter and Easter Monday, Liberation Day (April 25), Labor Day (May 1), Anniversary of the Republic (Sunday closest to June 2), Assumption of the Virgin (August 15), All Saints' Day (November 1), Feast of the Immaculate Conception (December 8), Christmas Day (December 25), St. Stephen's Day (December 26)

The Colosseum was a 50,000-seat stadium used for gladiator fights in ancient Rome. The name Colosseum comes from *Colosso di Nerone*, a statue of the Emperor Nero that stood near the stadium.

Timeline

900 BCE	The Etruscans establish themselves north of the Tiber River
753 BCE	Romulus and Remus found Rome, according to legend
500s BCE	The Etruscans control what is now northern Italy, while Greek colonies control the south
510 BCE	Rome becomes a **Republic**
27 BCE	Augustus is the first Roman Emperor
96–180 CE	The Roman **Empire** is at its most powerful
C. 350 CE onward	Invasion from German **tribes**
395 CE	The Roman Empire splits in two
C. 1300	The **Renaissance** begins in Tuscany
1469–1492	Lorenzo the Magnificent, a member of the Medici family, rules Florence and commissions Leonardo da Vinci and Michelangelo, among other artists
1796	Napoleon Bonaparte conquers Italy
1815	Italy is released from French rule after Napoleon is defeated
1861	Kingdom of Italy is formed with Turin as the capital
1870	Rome becomes the capital of Italy
1871	Italy becomes a **unified** (single) country
1914–1918	World War I. Italy is on the side of the **Allies**.

1922	Mussolini becomes prime minister
1929	The Vatican is created as an independent **state**
1939–1945	World War II. Italy fights on the side of Germany.
1943	Italy surrenders to the Allies
1945	Mussolini is murdered
1946	The Republic of Italy is established
1957	Italy becomes a founding member of the European Economic Community, which later becomes the **European Union**
1978	Ex-prime minister Aldo Moro is kidnapped and murdered
1984	The Roman Catholic religion is no longer the official religion of Italy
2002	The Italian **currency**, the lira, is replaced by the euro
2006	Italy wins the soccer World Cup for the fourth time
2001	Silvio Berlusconi becomes prime minister for the third time
2008	Garbage is dumped on the streets of Naples due to problems with waste management
2008–2009	Global financial crisis puts Italy into a **recession**
2009	Earthquake in the Abruzzo region kills hundreds of people and leaves many without homes

Glossary

Allies countries that fought against Germany during the World Wars. The Allies included Great Britain, France, and the United States.

architecture style of building

assembly law-making body, part of the Italian parliament

birth rate number of births per person

breeding bearing offspring; a word usually used for animals or birds

carnival celebration in which people wear costumes and feast on delicious foods

citizen person who belongs to a country and is part of its society. You have to be a citizen of a country to be able to vote in political elections.

civilization society in which a high level of culture, science, and government has been reached

congestion charge charge paid by drivers to enter a certain part of a city

corruption dishonest activity, particularly by people in positions of power in government

culture practices, traditions, and beliefs of a society

currency banknotes and coins accepted in exchange for goods and services

dubbed when a new soundtrack is added to a film, usually in a different language

economy to do with money and the industry and jobs in a country

elect choose by voting. The public elects a person to represent them in parliament.

empire group of countries ruled by a single powerful country

endangered in danger of extinction

erupt burst out suddenly and violently. When a volcano erupts, lava explodes from an opening at its top.

export sell goods to another country

European Union (EU) political and economic union of (currently) 27 European countries

head of state main public representative of a country, such as a queen or president

Holy Roman Empire large empire in Europe that began with the crowning of a German king as Holy Roman Emperor in 962 CE, and is thought to have ended in 1806. The emperor ruled over various parts of Europe at different times.

import buy goods from another country

industrialized when a place relies on industry rather than agriculture for its living

landfill site place where garbage is buried underground

national curriculum plan for what subjects will be taught in all schools in a country

nationalist person who supports and has a strong belief in his or her own country

peninsula long, thin piece of land that sticks out into the sea

pope leader of the Roman Catholic Church

recession when economic activity slows, unemployment often rises, and interest rates fall, over a period of time

Renaissance revival of art and literature in a style similar to that of ancient Greece and Rome

republic country with an elected leader and no king or queen

resource means available for a country to develop, such as minerals and energy sources

rural in the countryside

species group of living things that have certain features in common and can breed together

stable settled

state nation or place where people of particular politics or culture are organized into a single group

trade buying and selling of goods, usually between countries

tribe independent social group, historically often made up of primitive or nomadic people

unification joining together

unified single

Find Out More

Books

Anderson, Robert. *Italy*. Washington, D.C.: National Geographic Children's
    Books, 2009.

Blashfield, Jean F. *Italy*. Danbury, CT: Children's Press, 2008.

Donaldson, Madeline. *Italy*. Minneapolis: Lerner Publications, 2010.

Green, Jen. *Focus on Italy*. New York: World Almanac Library, 2007.

Hardyman, Robyn. *Italy*. New York: Chelsea House Publications, 2009.

McCulloch, Julie. *Italy* (A World of Recipes). Chicago: Heinemann-Raintree,
    2009.

Powell, Jillian. *Looking at Italy*. New York: Gareth Stevens Publishing, 2007.

Simmons, Walter. *Italy*. Minneapolis: Bellwether Media, 2010.

Websites

dsc.discovery.com/convergence/pompeii/pompeii.html

Try making a virtual volcano as well as learning more about the devastating
eruption at Pompeii.

kids.nationalgeographic.com/kids/places/find/italy

This website tells you more about the country of Italy.

www.bbc.co.uk/history/ancient/romans/launch_gms_gladiator.shtml

On this website you can try dressing a gladiator so that he can win his fight!

www.bbc.co.uk/history/historic_figures

This website has biographies of many of the people mentioned in this book.
You can find out more about Caesar, Napoleon, and Michelangelo.

**https://www.cia.gov/library/publications/the-world-factbook/geos/
it.html**

The website of the CIA World Factbook provides a lot of good report

information on Italy.

Places to visit

If you ever get the chance to go to Italy, these are some of the places you could visit:

Bologna

If you visit this city you should eat some spaghetti Bolognese!

The Colosseum in Rome

Imagine being a gladiator at the Colosseum!

Florence

Visit the Accademia gallery to see Michelangelo's statue of David.

The Greek Temples at Agrigento

Go back in time and visit these ancient Greek temples.

The Leaning Tower of Pisa

Have your photo taken propping up the Leaning Tower!

Milan

You could go and watch one of Milan's famous soccer teams play.

Pompeii

Discover the ruins of a Roman town destroyed by the eruption of Mount Vesuvius in 79 CE.

Siena

Visit this city to watch the Palio in July or August.

Venice

Travel in a gondola or climb the Campanile bell tower.

Topic Tools

You can use these topic tools for your school projects. Trace the map onto a sheet of paper, using the thick black outline to guide you.

The Italian flag was created by Napoleon Bonaparte in 1796 after he had conquered Italy for France. Napoleon chose to replace the blue panel of the French flag with a panel in his favorite color, green. Copy the flag design and then color in your picture. Make sure you use the right colors!

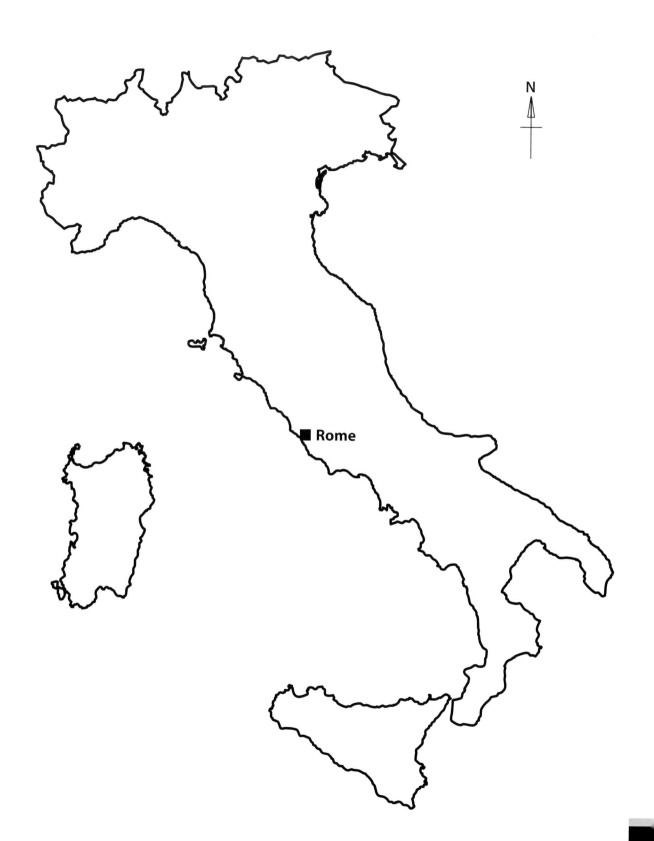

N

Rome

Index

Titles in the series